STATE PROFILES

TEXAS

BY PATRICK PERISH

BLASTOFF! DISCOVERY

BELLWETHER MEDIA • MINNEAPOLIS, MN

Blastoff! Discovery launches a new mission: reading to learn. Filled with facts and features, each book offers you an exciting new world to explore!

BLASTOFF! UNIVERSE

BLASTOFF! Beginners — GRADE K

BLASTOFF! READERS — GRADES 1-3

DISCOVERY — GRADE 4

This edition first published in 2022 by Bellwether Media, Inc.

No part of this publication may be reproduced in whole or in part without written permission of the publisher.
For information regarding permission, write to Bellwether Media, Inc.,
Attention: Permissions Department,
6012 Blue Circle Drive, Minnetonka, MN 55343.

Library of Congress Cataloging-in-Publication Data

Names: Perish, Patrick, author.
Title: Texas / by Patrick Perish.
Other titles: Blastoff! discovery. State profiles.
Description: Minneapolis, MN : Bellwether Media, Inc., 2022. |
  Series: Blastoff! discovery : State profiles | Includes bibliographical
  references and index. | Audience: Ages 7-13 | Audience: Grades 4-6 |
  Summary: "Engaging images accompany information about Texas.
  The combination of high-interest subject matter and narrative text is
  intended for students in grades 3 through 8"–Provided by publisher.
Identifiers: LCCN 2021019580 (print) | LCCN 2021019581 (ebook) |
  ISBN 9781644873496 (library binding) | ISBN 9781648341922 (ebook)
Subjects: LCSH: Texas–Juvenile literature. | CYAC: Texas. | LCGFT:
  Instructional and educational works.
Classification: LCC F386.3 .P455 2022 (print) | LCC F386.3 (ebook) |
  DDC 976.4–dc23
LC record available at https://lccn.loc.gov/2021019580
LC ebook record available at https://lccn.loc.gov/2021019581

Editor: Colleen Sexton   Designer: Jeffrey Kollock

Printed in the United States of America, North Mankato, MN.

TABLE OF CONTENTS

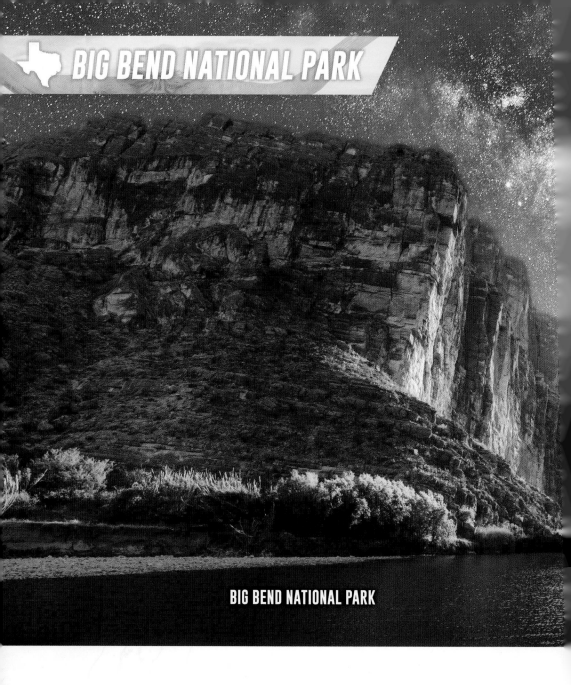

BIG BEND NATIONAL PARK

The evening brings a cool breeze to Big Bend National Park. A ranger hops in her truck and heads out to patrol. She winds around the Chisos Mountains past pine and juniper forests. A cougar sprints across the road. Farther on, she passes grasslands and rocky ridges.

STARRY NIGHTS

Big Bend National Park is a great place for stargazing. Because it lies far from city lights, the night skies there are among the darkest in North America.

ALAMO MISSION

GUADALUPE MOUNTAINS

PALO DURO CANYON

SOUTH PADRE ISLAND

The ranger comes to a trail at the west end of the park. She leaves her truck and hikes into Santa Elena **Canyon**. There, the Rio Grande flows between towering rock walls. She hikes back out of the canyon just as the first stars appear in the sky. Welcome to Texas!

NEW MEXICO

● EL PASO

Texas is in the south-central United States. The Rio Grande flows along its southwestern border with Mexico. New Mexico borders Texas to the northwest. Texas's neighbor to the north is Oklahoma. Its eastern edge meets Arkansas and Louisiana. The **Gulf** of Mexico washes against the state's long southeastern shoreline.

As the second-largest state, Texas covers 268,596 square miles (695,660 square kilometers). The state's highest point, Guadalupe Peak, stands 8,749 feet (2,667 meters) high in western Texas. Austin is the state capital. It sits on the Colorado River in south-central Texas. Other major cities include Houston, San Antonio, and Dallas.

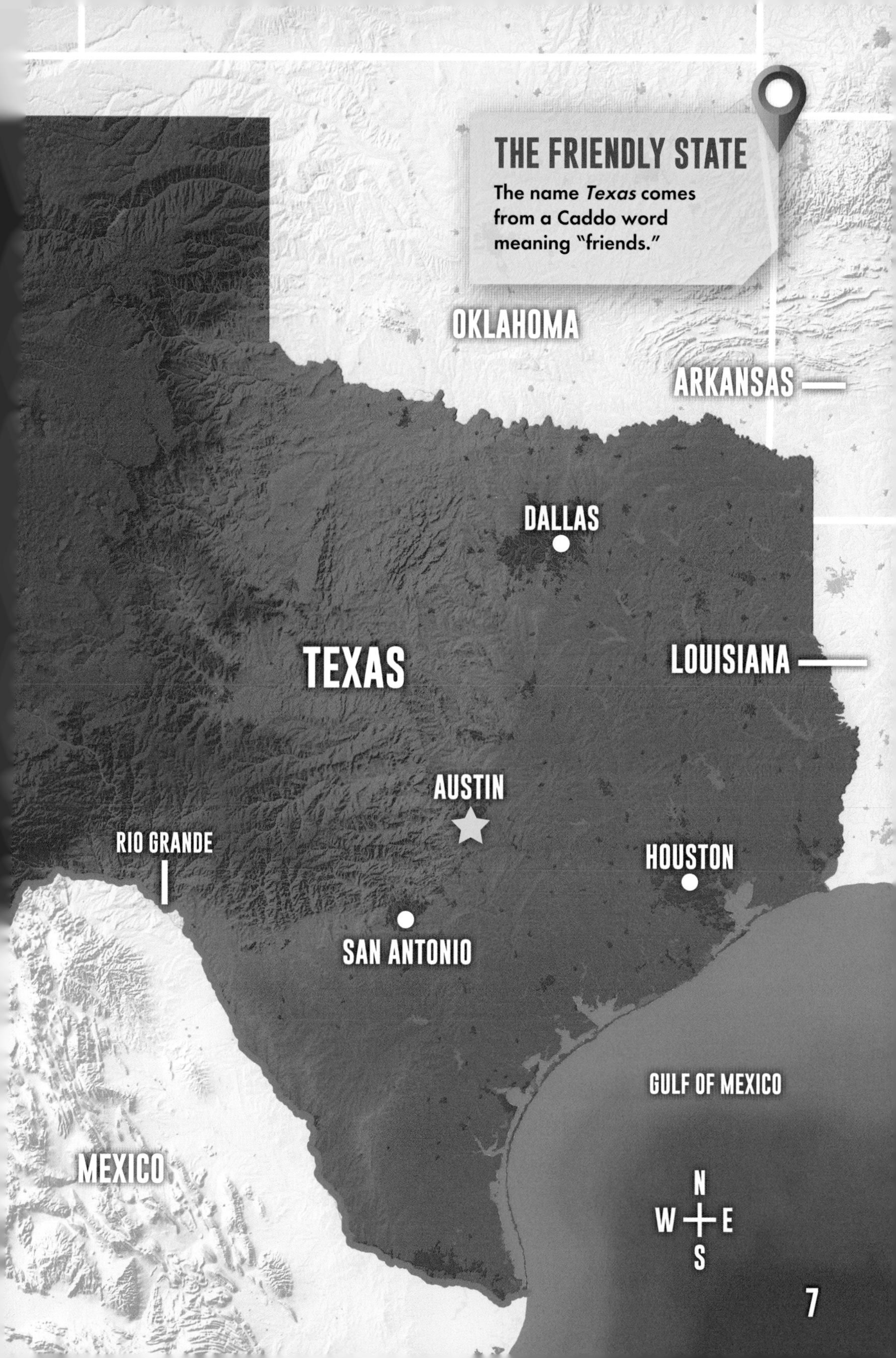

OKLAHOMA
ARKANSAS
DALLAS
TEXAS
LOUISIANA
AUSTIN
RIO GRANDE
HOUSTON
SAN ANTONIO
GULF OF MEXICO
MEXICO
N
W
E
S

THE FRIENDLY STATE

The name *Texas* comes from a Caddo word meaning "friends."

THE ALAMO
SAN ANTONIO

CATTLE DRIVES

Texas's open plains drew cowboys to help raise cattle for beef. From the 1860s to the 1890s, cowboys drove Texas longhorns north to be shipped from railroad centers. They herded around 3,000 cattle on each drive!

People have lived in Texas for thousands of years. In the 1500s, the Spanish explored Texas. They met Native American groups, including the Caddo, Karankawa, Apache, and Comanche. Spanish priests arrived in the late 1600s. They established the Alamo and many other **missions**. They worked to spread Christianity to Native Americans.

In 1821, Texas came under Mexico's rule. Texas broke away from Mexico in 1836. It was an independent country until it became the 28th state in 1845. During the **Civil War**, Texas fought for the South. After the war, the government pushed most Native Americans out of Texas.

NATIVE PEOPLES OF TEXAS

TIGUA INDIANS OF YSLETA DEL SUR PUEBLO

- Original lands in New Mexico
- Came to western Texas in 1680 after conflicts with the Spanish
- Over 4,000 in Texas today

ALABAMA-COUSHATTA TRIBE

- Original lands in Alabama
- Settled in eastern Texas by 1780
- Over 1,200 in Texas today

KICKAPOO TRADITIONAL TRIBE OF TEXAS

- Original lands around the Great Lakes states of Wisconsin, Michigan, and Illinois
- Came to Texas in the 1800s
- About 960 in Texas today

Salt marshes and **sandbars** protect the southeastern Texas coast. The flat Gulf Coastal **Plain** stretches from the **bayous** and **thickets** of the northeastern Piney Woods to the rich soil of the Rio Grande Valley. The high, flat land of the **Great Plains** stretches across central Texas. Hills roll across the north. Texas's western corner features dry plains, river **gorges**, and rugged peaks, including the tall Guadalupe Mountains.

RIO GRANDE

GULF COASTAL PLAIN
GREAT PLAINS
GUADALUPE MOUNTAINS

N
W + E
S

RIO GRANDE
BIG BEND NATIONAL PARK

HOT AND COLD

In January, it is not unusual for temperatures to reach 90 degrees Fahrenheit (32 degrees Celsius) in southern Texas. At the same time, freezing blizzards can strike northern Texas.

SEASONAL HIGHS AND LOWS

SPRING
HIGH: 78°F (26°C)
LOW: 56°F (13°C)

SUMMER
HIGH: 91°F (33°C)
LOW: 72°F (22°C)

FALL
HIGH: 78°F (26°C)
LOW: 57°F (14°C)

WINTER
HIGH: 61°F (16°C)
LOW: 38°F (3°C)

°F = degrees Fahrenheit
°C = degrees Celsius

BAYOU
CADDO LAKE

The climate varies across Texas. Eastern Texas is hot and wet. Western Texas receives less rain. Tornadoes, dust storms, and blizzards blast across the northwest. Powerful **hurricanes** sometimes batter the coast.

ROSEATE SPOONBILL

Texas's landscapes provide homes for a wide variety of wildlife. Spoonbills wade in coastal waters to hunt for crayfish. In eastern Texas, alligators lurk in overgrown swamps. Squirrels chatter from loblolly pines. Armadillos waddle through fields of bluebonnets that buzz with bees. Screech owls bring Texas blind snakes to their nests to eat.

In the northern plains, prairie dogs bark from their underground homes. They duck inside as golden eagles swoop by. Rattlesnakes rest under prickly pear cactuses. The deserts of Big Bend come alive at night. Scorpions and tarantulas crawl over rocks. Coyotes yip and prowl.

NINE-BANDED ARMADILLO

EASTERN SCREECH OWL

WESTERN DIAMONDBACK RATTLESNAKE

COYOTE

THE STATE REPTILE

Texas horned lizards are also called horny toads. These spiky lizards eat ants. They squirt blood from their eyes when they feel threatened!

TEXAS HORNED LIZARD

Life Span: at least 5 years
Status: least concern

Texas horned lizard range = ■

LEAST CONCERN	NEAR THREATENED	VULNERABLE	ENDANGERED	CRITICALLY ENDANGERED	EXTINCT IN THE WILD	EXTINCT
▲						

About 29 million people live in Texas. Around 9 of every 10 live in or near cities. Texas has a strong Hispanic **heritage**. More than one-third of Texans identify as Hispanic. Hispanic Texans often call themselves Tejanos.

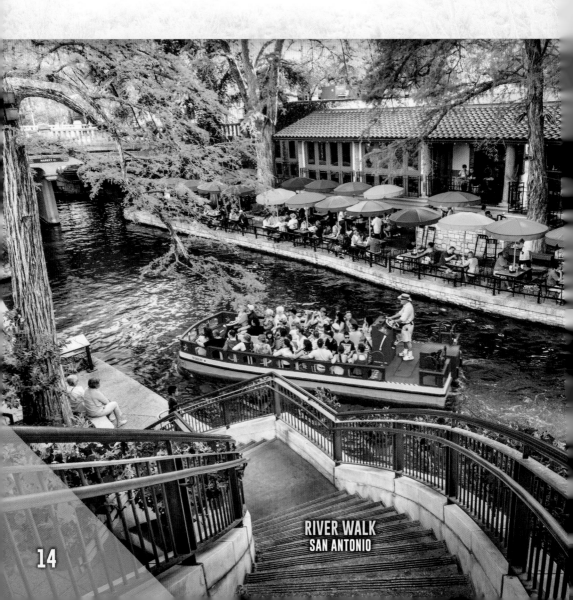

RIVER WALK
SAN ANTONIO

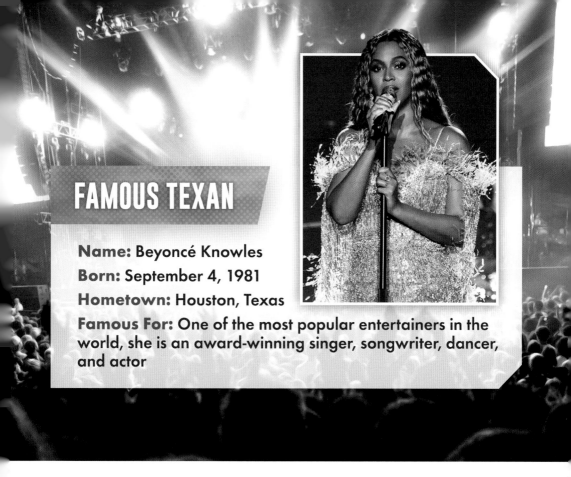

FAMOUS TEXAN

Name: Beyoncé Knowles
Born: September 4, 1981
Hometown: Houston, Texas
Famous For: One of the most popular entertainers in the world, she is an award-winning singer, songwriter, dancer, and actor

Fewer than half of Texans have European roots. Many have German, Irish, or Czech backgrounds. One in eight Texans is African American or Black. Smaller numbers are Asian American or Native American. The state's three **reservations** belong to the Alabama-Coushatta, Kickapoo, and Tigua tribes. **Immigrants** from Mexico, Honduras, El Salvador, India, and China also call Texas home.

TEXAS'S FUTURE: SMALL TOWNS

As cities in Texas grow, many small towns are shrinking. Keeping schools, businesses, and hospitals open in some areas has become a challenge. State and local governments will need to find ways to keep services available to all Texans.

HOUSTON

Located in southeastern Texas, Houston is Texas's largest city. Founded in 1836, Houston became a port and early trading center. Today it is an important center for **refining** oil and producing chemicals. Houston's downtown skyline is one of the tallest in the country. Hikers and bikers enjoy trails in the city's many parks.

JOHNSON SPACE CENTER

SPACE VEHICLE MOCKUP FACILITY

HOME OF ASTRONAUT TRAINING

SPACE CITY

Houston's Johnson Space Center is an astronaut training center. From there, NASA's Mission Control Center guided the first moon landing in 1969.

Houston is a **diverse** city with large African American, Black, Asian American, and Hispanic populations. Popular festivals celebrate Greek, Korean, Polish, and Japanese **cultures**. Residents head to Houston's downtown theater district to see local ballet, opera, and orchestra performances. The city also boasts more than 150 museums.

Texas has more farms and ranches than any other state. It leads the nation in beef and cotton production. The Rio Grande Valley is an important growing region. There, farmers tend to citrus orchards and pecan trees. Throughout the state, farmers harvest watermelons, strawberries, and spinach. Fishing crews haul in fish and shrimp from Gulf waters.

TEXAS'S CHALLENGE: CLEAN AIR

Texas's refineries and chemical plants are important industries. But they increase air pollution. High levels of air pollution can make residents sick. Finding ways to keep the air clean is an important goal for the state.

Texas is the nation's largest oil and **petrochemical** producer. It also leads the country in natural gas and wind power. Texas is the second-largest **manufacturing** state. Factory workers produce chemicals, electronics, and processed meats. Most Texans have **service jobs**. They work in restaurants, hotels, banks, and schools.

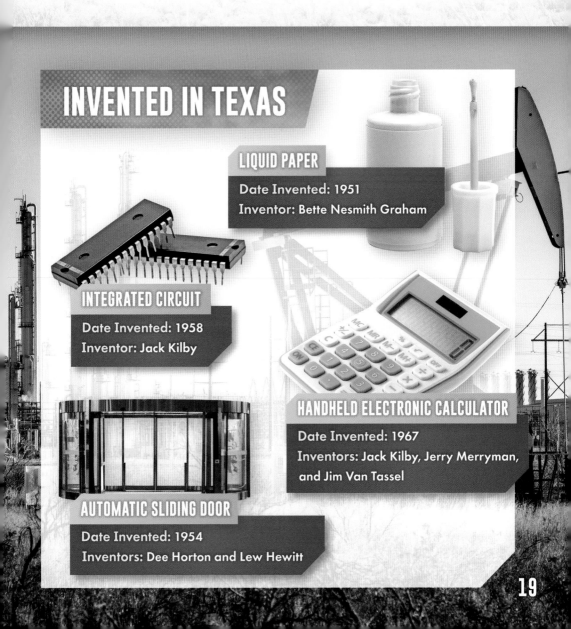

INVENTED IN TEXAS

LIQUID PAPER
Date Invented: 1951
Inventor: Bette Nesmith Graham

INTEGRATED CIRCUIT
Date Invented: 1958
Inventor: Jack Kilby

HANDHELD ELECTRONIC CALCULATOR
Date Invented: 1967
Inventors: Jack Kilby, Jerry Merryman, and Jim Van Tassel

AUTOMATIC SLIDING DOOR
Date Invented: 1954
Inventors: Dee Horton and Lew Hewitt

FAJITAS

Tex-Mex dishes are popular in Texas. They blend Mexican and Texan cooking. Fajitas feature grilled strips of steak and vegetables on flour tortillas. In the late 1800s, the Chili Queens of San Antonio made *chili con carne* popular. These local women served this chili with beef, garlic, cumin, and peppers from street stalls. True Texas chili does not have beans.

RUBY REDS

Ruby red grapefruit is the state fruit of Texas. The dark red variety was discovered in southern Texas in 1929. These popular fruits are shipped worldwide.

Texans take barbecue seriously. Texas-style barbecue is beef with salt and pepper smoked over an oak fire. It does not have sauce. Kolaches are popular Czech pastries filled with fruit or sausages. Pecans star in the state dessert, pecan pie.

BARBECUE

KOLACHES

NACHOS

2-4 SERVINGS

Have an adult help you make this popular snack!

INGREDIENTS

2 cups tortilla chips

1 1/2 cups refried beans

1 1/2 cups cheddar cheese, grated

2 pickled jalapeño peppers, sliced

salsa

sour cream

guacamole

DIRECTIONS

1. Preheat the oven to 350 degrees Fahrenheit (177 degrees Celsius).

2. Arrange the tortilla chips in the bottom of a wide, shallow baking pan.

3. Spread the refried beans over the chips.

4. Sprinkle the cheese and jalapeño peppers on top.

5. Bake for 10 minutes, or until the cheese is melted.

6. Serve hot with salsa, sour cream, and guacamole.

BULL-RIDING

Sports are big in Texas! Many Texans play basketball or baseball. High school football games draw huge crowds. Fans cheer for professional teams such as the Dallas Cowboys, San Antonio Spurs, and Houston Astros. Fishing and hunting are popular outdoor sports. The Gulf coast offers sandy beaches and sailing. Rodeos highlight Texas's ranching heritage. Texans compete in bull-riding and cattle-roping.

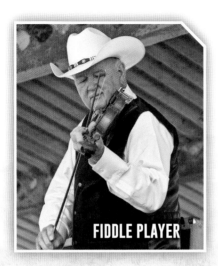
FIDDLE PLAYER

Texas is home to artists and performers of all styles. Craftspeople are known for their pottery, quilts, and saddles. Residents enjoy lively Tejano music. It blends Mexican, American, and European styles. Fiddle contests and music festivals showcase the state's country music roots.

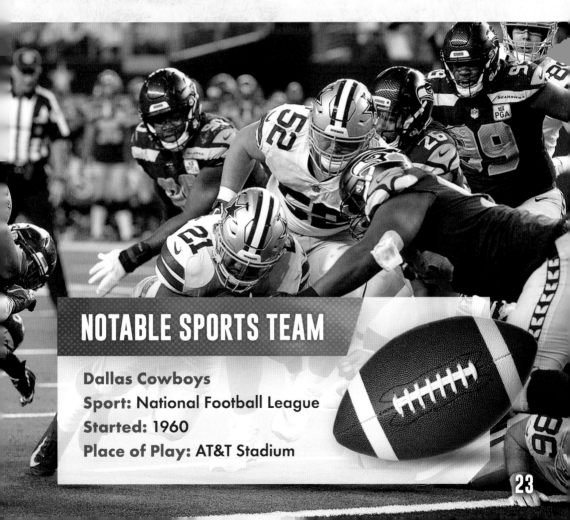

NOTABLE SPORTS TEAM

Dallas Cowboys
Sport: National Football League
Started: 1960
Place of Play: AT&T Stadium

Texans know how to celebrate! The town of Terlingua hosts an annual chili cook-off. Chefs have battled there for over 50 years. Big Tex, an enormous cowboy statue, greets visitors every year at the Texas State Fair.

Texans celebrate Juneteenth with parades, picnics, and dancing. It marks the day in 1865 that **enslaved** African Americans in Texas were told that they were free. Brownsville and the neighboring Mexican city of Matamoros hold Charro Days. This festival celebrates the friendship between the two nations. San Antonio's Texas Folklife Festival showcases the food and crafts of over 40 cultures. These events bring together Texans of all backgrounds!

CHARRO DAYS

TEXAS STATE FAIR

1836

The Republic of Texas wins its independence and becomes an independent country

500-1500

Native American groups in Texas begin farming

1821

Mexico gains its independence from Spain and takes control of Texas

1519

Spanish explorer Alonso Alvarez de Piñeda maps the Texas coast

1690-1790

Spanish priests establish missions across Texas to convert Native Americans to Christianity

1865

On June 19, enslaved African Americans in Texas are told that they are free

1969

NASA's Mission Control Center in Houston guides the Apollo 11 landing on the moon

2017

Hurricane Harvey causes billions of dollars in damage in Texas and Louisiana

1963

President John F. Kennedy is shot and killed in Dallas, leading Texan Lyndon Johnson to be sworn in as president

2000

Texas governor George W. Bush is elected the 43rd president of the United States

1845

Texas becomes the 28th state

TEXAS FACTS

Nickname: The Lone Star State

Motto: Friendship

Date of Statehood: December 29, 1845 (the 28th state)

Capital City: Austin ★

Other Major Cities: Houston, San Antonio, Dallas, Fort Worth, El Paso

Area: 268,596 square miles (695,660 square kilometers); Texas is the 2nd largest state.

Population

29,145,505
(2020)

STATE FLAG

Adopted in 1839, Texas's state flag is known as the Lone Star Flag. On the left, a white star appears on a vertical blue stripe. A red stripe and a white stripe are on the right. White stands for purity, and blue is a symbol for loyalty. Red represents bravery.

INDUSTRY

Main Exports

oil

electronic parts

aircraft parts

natural gas

cotton

machinery

JOBS

MANUFACTURING
6%

FARMING AND NATURAL RESOURCES
5%

GOVERNMENT
12%

SERVICES
77%

Natural Resources
oil, natural gas, coal, salt, soil

GOVERNMENT

Federal Government

38 REPRESENTATIVES | **2** SENATORS

40 ELECTORAL VOTES

USA

TX

State Government

150 REPRESENTATIVES | **31** SENATORS

STATE SYMBOLS

STATE BIRD
MOCKINGBIRD

STATE ANIMAL
TEXAS LONGHORN

STATE FLOWER
BLUEBONNET

STATE TREE
PECAN

GLOSSARY

bayous—slow-moving streams of water in marshy areas

canyon—a deep and narrow valley that has steep sides

Civil War—a war between the Northern (Union) and Southern (Confederate) states that lasted from 1861 to 1865

cultures—beliefs, arts, and ways of life in places or societies

diverse—made up of people from many different backgrounds

enslaved—to be considered property and forced to work for no pay

gorges—narrow canyons with steep walls

Great Plains—a region of flat or gently rolling land in the central United States

gulf—part of an ocean or sea that extends into land

heritage—the traditions, achievements, and beliefs that are part of the history of a group of people

hurricanes—storms formed in the tropics that have violent winds and often have rain and lightning

immigrants—people who move to a new country

manufacturing—a field of work in which people use machines to make products

missions—places where people live while spreading a religious faith

petrochemical—a chemical that comes from oil or natural gas

plain—a large area of flat land

refining—making a substance pure

reservations—areas of land that are controlled by Native American tribes

sandbars—long mounds of sand that tides and currents form in the water

service jobs—jobs that perform tasks for people or businesses

thickets—small, thick patches of low trees or bushes

AT THE LIBRARY

DeRubertis, Barbara. *Let's Celebrate Emancipation Day & Juneteenth*. New York, N.Y.: Kane Press, 2018.

Gregory, Josh. *Texas*. New York, N.Y.: Children's Press, 2018.

Ryckman, Tatiana. *Texas*. New York, N.Y.: Cavendish Square, 2020.

ON THE WEB

FACTSURFER

Factsurfer.com gives you a safe, fun way to find more information.

1. Go to www.factsurfer.com.

2. Enter "Texas" into the search box and click 🔍.

3. Select your book cover to see a list of related content.

INDEX

The images in this book are reproduced through the courtesy of: shutterstock, front cover, p. 28 (flag); railway fx, p. 3; Stanley Ford, pp. 4-5; Sean Pavone, pp. 5 (Alamo), 16 (inset); Anton Foltin, p. 5 (Guadalupe); xradiophotog, p. 5 (Palo Duro); Hundley Photography, p. 5 (South Padre Island); Svineyard, p. 8; patti jean_images, p. 8 (fun fact); Martina Birnbn p. 9; Inge Johnsson/ Alamy, p. 10; amadeustx, p. 11; Pi-Lens, p. 11 (inset); Audrey Snider-Bell, p. 12 (snake); Bonnie Tayl Barry, p. 12 (spoonbill); Artiom Photo, p. 12 (armadillo); Mircea Costina, p. 12 (owl); Warren Metcalf, p. 12 (coyote); Bill Gorum/ Alamy, p. 13; dszc, pp. 14, 19; Media Union, p. 15; Kevin Mazur/ Getty Images, p. 15 (inset); Nate Hovee p. 16; Kumar Sriskandan/ Alamy, p. 17; M.Aurelius, p. 17 (fun fact); Sara Carpenter, p. 18; fotoslaz, p. 18 (fun fact); Mega Pixel, p. 19 (liquid paper); Ragnarock, p. 19 (circuit); Nor Gal, p. 19 (calculator); Sorranop, p. 19 (door); Joshua Resnick, pp. 20, 21 (barbecue); Brent Hofacker, p. 20 (fun fact); pbd Studio, p. 21 (kolaches); Nina Firsova, p. 2' Olga Miltsova, p. 21 (inset); alan turkington/ Alamy, p. 22; Stephen Saks Photography/ Alamy, p. 23 (fiddle); Fort Wort Star-Telegram/ Getty Images, p. 23; bestv, p. 23 (football); Roberto Galan, p. 24; Donovan Reese Photography/ Getty Images, p. 23; PhotoFires, p. 26 (1690); Ludovicus Ferdinandus/ Wikipedia, p. 26 (1821); Ryan Conine, pp. 26-3 (background); Digital Images Studio, p. 27 (1969); Eric Draper/ Wikipedia, p. 27 (2000); Gerald A. DeBoer, p. 29 (bir Quinn Calder, p. 29 (animal); NicholasGeraldinePhotos, p. 29 (flower); Itsik Marom, p. 29 (tree); Margo Harrison, p. 31